CONTENTS

Words in **bold** are explained in the glossary.

Fun at the park

It is fun to go to the park.

I a... ...ng

...Park

Editorial consultant: Mitch Cronick

There is always lots to do.

Spring in the park

It is **spring**.

There is lots to see.

Green leaves

Daffodils

Flower buds

Spring ducklings

The ducks lay eggs in the spring.

The ducklings **hatch** from the eggs.

Duck

Ducklings

9

Summer in the park

You can have a picnic in the **summer**.

11

At the playground

You can go to the playground.

Slide

12

Swing

13

Autumn fun

It is **autumn**.

The leaves fall off the trees.

Leaves

15

Autumn seeds

The trees have **seeds**.

You can collect them.

Acorn

Winter in the park

You can play football in the **winter**.

Playing football will keep you warm!

Snow!

It snows in winter.

You can make a snowman.

Snowman

21

Glossary

autumn
We divide a year into spring, summer, autumn and winter. Autumn is when trees drop their leaves and the weather gets cool.

hatch
To break out of an egg.

seeds
Small parts of plants that will grow into new plants.

spring

We divide a year into spring, summer, autumn and winter. Spring is when new plants grow. Lots of animals have babies in spring.

summer

We divide a year into spring, summer, autumn and winter. Summer is when the weather gets warmer.

winter

We divide a year into spring, summer, autumn and winter. Winter is when plants die off and the weather gets colder.

Index

Publisher: Melissa Fairley
Art Director: Faith Booker
Editor: Emma Dods
Designer: Simon Fenn
Production Controller: Ed Green
Production Manager: Suzy Kelly

ISBN: 978 1 84898 230 7

Copyright © TickTock Entertainment Ltd 2010
First published in Great Britain in 2010 by TickTock Entertainment Ltd,
The Old Sawmill, 103 Goods Station Road, Tunbridge Wells, Kent, TN1 2DP

Printed in China
1 3 5 7 9 10 8 6 4 2

Picture credits (t=top, b=bottom, c=centre, l=left, r=right, OFC=outside front cover, OBC=outside back cover):
AFP/Getty Images: 6–7. BrandX/www.photolibrary.com: 18–19. iStock: 1, 8t, 16, 20–21, 22t.
Shutterstock: OFC, Flap, 2, 4–5 (all), 7t, 8–9, 10–11, 12, 13, 14–15 (all), 17, 20, 22b, 23t, OBC.

Every effort has been made to trace the copyright holders, and we apologize in advance for any unintentional omissions.
We would be pleased to insert the appropriate acknowledgements in any subsequent edition of this publication.

24